ENDANGERED!

LIONS

Amanda Harman

Series Consultant: James G. Doherty
General Curator, The Bronx Zoo, New York

BENCHMARK BOOKS

MARSHALL CAVENDISH
NEW YORK

Benchmark Books
Marshall Cavendish Corporation
99 White Plains Road
Tarrytown, New York 10591-9001

Library of Congress Cataloging-in-Publication Data

Harman, Amanda, 1968-
　　Lions / by Amanda Harman.
　　　　p.　　cm. — (Endangered!)
　　Includes index.
　　Summary: Describes the physical characteristics, habitat, and
behavior of African and Asiatic lions, why attitudes toward them
have changed, and how their numbers are increasing.
　　ISBN 0-7614-0291-8
　　1. Lions—Juvenile literature. 2. Endangered species—Juvenile
literature.　　[1. Lions. 2. Endangered species.] I. Title.
II. Series.
QL737.C23H3575　1997
599.74'428—dc20　　　　　　　　　　　　　　　　　96-7219
　　　　　　　　　　　　　　　　　　　　　　　　　　CIP
　　　　　　　　　　　　　　　　　　　　　　　　　　AC

Printed and bound in the United States

PICTURE CREDITS
*The publishers would like to thank the Frank Lane Picture Agency for
supplying all the photographs used in this book except for the following:* 14,
20, 25, 29 Ardea; 12, 13, 18, 19 Bruce Coleman Ltd; 4, 6 Andy Rouse.

Series created by Brown Packaging

Front cover: African lion.
Title page: Lioness with cub.
Back cover: Lioness with cubs.

Contents

The male lion's mane makes him unmistakable. The lion is the second largest cat in the world, after the Siberian tiger.

Introduction

The lion is perhaps the most famous of all wild animals. Throughout the world, many different peoples think of the lion as brave and wise. And with his long, flowing mane and loud, ferocious roar, the male lion – often called the "king of the beasts" – is truly majestic.

Lions are cats, like tigers and leopards and the pet cats that many of us keep at home. Lions have a stocky, muscular body, fairly short legs, and large, powerful paws. Males lions may reach almost 14 feet (4.3 m) from nose to tail-tip. The heaviest of them can weigh as much as 550 pounds (250 kg). Female lions, called lionesses, are smaller. They may grow to 12 feet (3.7 m) long.

Lions are the only cats to have a big, dark tuft on the end of their tail. The lion's coat varies in color from a light sandy yellow to a golden tawny brown on the back and

A lioness in east Africa. Young lions' coats have spots. These fade as the cats get older, but sometimes do not vanish altogether.

sides, and is lighter, almost white, on the chest and belly. The male lion has a large, bushy mane, which covers the top of his head, his cheeks, and his throat. Some older lions have extra-long manes that reach all the way down to their chest. As a lion gets older, its mane may get darker and darker, until it is almost black, with just a few golden streaks. For this reason, some old males are known as "black-maned lions."

In the past, people who shared their land with lions thought these cats were magical creatures, and they

This lion's mane covers much of his body. Manes make lions look bigger than they are, which helps to frighten off enemies.

worshiped them as if they were gods. Sadly, because lions were seen as strong, courageous, and intelligent, hunters thought it a great challenge to kill them. They then displayed their heads or skins as trophies. As a result, huge numbers of lions were wiped out, and in many parts of the world they became endangered or completely **extinct**.

In this book, we will learn all about lions. In particular, we will see how people's attitudes toward these beautiful cats have changed over the years, and look at what is being done to prevent lions from disappearing in the wild.

A lioness tries to rest while her two cubs pester her. Lions may live up to 15 years in the wild and may reach 24 in zoos.

Where Lions Live

In prehistoric times, lions were among the most widespread **mammals** in the world. Their **range** covered most of the northern half of the world and parts of South America as well. Now lions are found only in Africa, from just south of the Sahara Desert to South Africa, and in a small area of northwestern India. There is only one **species** of lion, but lions from different areas differ slightly from one another. Scientists look at them as a number of **subspecies**.

A family of Barbary lions. The Barbary lion is extinct in the wild, but some still live in zoos. On the right is a young male.

There were once seven different subspecies of lions in the world. However, today the Barbary lion (which once lived in northern Africa) is extinct in the wild, and the Cape lion (which once lived in South Africa) is totally extinct. There are just five subspecies left: the Angolan, Masai, Senegalese, Transvaal, and Asiatic lions. The Angolan lion lives in Zimbabwe, Angola, and Zaire in central Africa. The Masai lion is found in east Africa. The Senegalese lion is found in west Africa. The Transvaal lion lives in the Transvaal region of South Africa.

Large numbers of Asiatic lions could once be found from Greece in southeastern Europe, and across the Middle

Areas where lions can be found

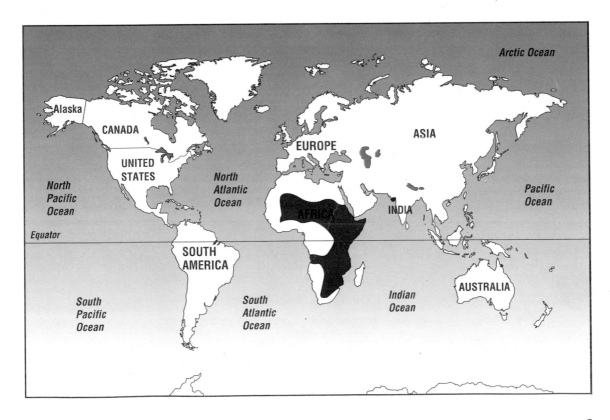

East to eastern India. Sadly, this subspecies is in very serious danger today. The remaining Asiatic lions live in a special **reserve** in the northwestern Indian state of Gujarat. This reserve is called the Gir Forest Sanctuary.

The Asiatic lion looks slightly different from its African relative. It is generally a little smaller – the male does not usually grow bigger than about 11 feet 6 inches (3.6 m) from head to tail nor weigh more than 440 pounds (200 kg). The Asiatic lion also has a shaggier coat and a larger tail tuft than does the African lion.

A male Asiatic lion. Asiatic lions' manes tend not to be as furry as those of their African cousins.

Lions are **adapted** to living in a number of different types of **habitats**. They generally make their homes in grasslands, such as those in the Serengeti National Park in east Africa. But they can also be found in **scrub** and open woodland, and the Asiatic lion's natural habitat is **tropical** forest. Some lions even live in the driest of deserts, such as the Kalahari Desert in southern Africa. With just a few dusty shrubs, thorn bushes, or small acacia (a-KAY-sha) trees scattered around, there is very little cover for the lions to shelter or hide in. But their yellow or golden-brown coat camouflages these cats well against the sand, stone, and grass, making them very difficult to spot.

A group of lions rests after a rain and dust storm in Botswana, southern Africa. See how well the lions' color matches their surroundings.

How Lions Live

Most cats live alone. Lions, though, are different. They live in groups called **prides** and are the only truly social cats. There may be up to 40 members in a pride, including up to 6 adult males and 4 to 12 adult females with their cubs. The adult females in a pride are related to one another – they usually spend all their life in the pride into which they were born. The adult males may also be related to one another, but they are never related to the females. They do not stay in one pride for their whole lifetime, but move from pride to pride.

Each pride has its own **territory**. Territories vary in size, depending on how many lions there are and how rich the

A pride of lions relaxes in the shade in the Masai Mara Game Reserve in the east African nation of Kenya.

area is in food and water. A small territory usually covers about 8 square miles (20 sq km), whereas a large one may be as big as 150 square miles (400 sq km).

The males' task is to defend their pride's territory against other lions. During the day, they leave scent marks at the edges of their territory by spraying urine or rubbing their face and tail against trees, bushes, and rocks. At night, they roar loudly and fiercely to warn passing lions that the area is occupied. Every two or three years, however, a new male or group of males will enter the territory and try to take over the pride. Then the rivals fight ferociously, sometimes

A male lion scent marks a tree in his territory with urine to warn other lions to keep out.

until one or more of them is seriously wounded or even killed. If the challengers win the fight, they take charge of the pride, and the defeated males are forced to leave and look for another pride. The new leaders immediately kill all the pride's cubs. This may seem cruel, but the leaders want the lionesses to **mate** with them and not spend their time looking after the offspring of their defeated rivals.

Though they fight other lions for control of the pride, males do not fight among themselves over females. When a male finds a lioness who is ready to mate with him, the two are left together undisturbed. Lionesses can have cubs once every two years. There is no particular breeding season for lions, and they can mate at any time of year.

A young cub playfully sinks its teeth into an adult male. Though males kill other lions' cubs when they take over a pride, they take great care of their own young and will put up with a lot from them.

Three or four months after mating, the lioness is ready to give birth to her cubs. First she finds a safe, warm place to shelter. This place is called her **lair** and is usually close to a waterhole. Here she gives birth to a litter of one to five cubs, which are blind and weigh nearly 4 pounds (2 kg). The cubs are completely helpless at this stage, and their mother defends them against attack from **predators**, such as leopards, spotted hyenas, and wild dogs. Despite their mothers' protection, however, as many as four out of every five lion cubs die before they are two years old.

For the first six months, the lioness feeds her cubs on her milk, and they grow very quickly. Because they are all related, the lionesses in a pride sometimes take turns

A female lion takes a nap while her cubs lie close by. Though she appears sound asleep, she would wake quickly if she sensed danger.

feeding the other females' cubs as well as their own. At about three months old, the cubs start to eat meat as well as drinking milk. By this time, they have begun to go on hunting trips with their mother, learning the skills they will need when they have to fend for themselves.

Young lion cubs are extremely playful, and their games help them to practice hunting and fighting techniques. They learn these techniques from watching their mother and the other lionesses and lions in the pride. The games include pouncing on their mother's tail tuft as if it were a small animal and attacking one another. Like pet cats, lions hold their claws in special slots in their paws when they are playing so that they do not hurt one another. Once the cubs

A group of cubs share a zebra with the lionesses that killed it. From an early age, cubs watch their mothers hunt. They are not big and strong enough to take part until they are about one year old, though.

are a little older, their mother may bring back live **prey** that she has caught but not killed. They can then practice their killing techniques on the real thing.

By the time her offspring are two years old, the mother is ready to mate again, and the young lions have learned everything they need to survive on their own. The male cubs are forced out to find other prides, so that they do not become rivals to the adult males in the pride into which they were born. Two or three young males usually gang up together so that they will have a better chance of defeating any other lions that they challenge. As we have seen, though, the young lionesses usually stay with their own pride, with their mother, aunts, cousins, and sisters. At three years of age, they are old enough to mate and have cubs of their own.

A lion cub creeps up on a much younger relative, which is unaware that it is about to be jumped on. Lion cub play is often training for the future. In this case, the larger cub is practicing its stalking skills.

How Lions Hunt

The male lions protect their pride from intruders, but it is the lionesses that do most of the hunting. Lions are **carnivores**, and it is no easy task to catch enough food for the whole pride. Each male needs to eat at least 15 pounds (7 kg) of meat a day to survive, and each female needs at least 10 pounds (5 kg). Then there are the older cubs to feed (very young ones drink only milk, as we have seen).

Unlike other cats, such as tigers and leopards, lionesses do not usually hunt alone. Instead they work in teams to catch large hoofed mammals such as zebras, buffaloes, and antelope, which will sometimes feed the whole pride. Since

A hunting lioness stalks her prey in the grasslands of the Samburu National Reserve in Kenya. Males rarely take part in hunts.

they hunt as a group, lions can target healthy animals, as well as the old or sick as other predators often do.

Lionesses usually hunt when it is just beginning to get dark. This makes it a little more difficult for their prey to spot them as they creep up on them through the long grass. The poor light at this time of the day is not a problem for the lionesses, however. They have very good eyesight and can see five or six times better than a person can.

When hunting animals that graze in a large herd, the lionesses stalk their prey silently and stealthily. Each

A hunting party of lionesses in the Masai Mara Game Reserve creeps up on a group of impala, a kind of antelope.

female has a fixed place within the hunting group, a bit like players do on a football team. Slowly, the cats spread out in a long line, with the lionesses at each end creeping farther forward than those in the middle. This causes the line to form a horseshoe shape around the unwary animals. Whenever the prey lift their heads to sniff the air or look in the hunters' direction, the lionesses freeze. They do not move again until the animals look away.

Once the cats are within about 60 feet (18 m) of their prey, one of the lionesses singles out a victim and rushes forward. The startled animals run for their lives, with the lioness bounding after her prey as fast as she can. Lionesses are fast over short distances and can reach speeds of 35 miles per hour (56 km/h). As she catches up

Once caught, a young wildebeest is no match for a gang of lionesses. Lions are fast, but many hoofed mammals are faster, and the cats must attack before their prey can gather speed.

with her prey, she rears up onto her hind legs and leaps forward, grabbing the animal with her massive paws and long, sharp claws. The frightened creature struggles to break free, but once the other lionesses have caught up and joined in, it does not have a chance. Together, they wrestle the animal to the ground so that the leading lioness can kill it. She does this by clamping her powerful jaws around its mouth or throat so that it cannot breathe.

A lioness kills her victim – a buffalo – by holding its mouth shut so that it cannot breathe.

Once the animal is dead, the pride can begin to feed. All the lions, including cubs, compete over the kill, and there is much squabbling. The male lions get most, since they are the strongest. This is where the saying "the lion's share" comes from. The cubs usually get the least. If prey is in short supply, the cubs may not get to eat anything, and many young lions starve to death.

After a kill, each lion must struggle to get as much food as it can.

When lions are hungry and there are not many large hoofed animals around, they will hunt smaller animals, such as birds and small mammals. These are a little easier to catch, and lions and lionesses usually stalk them alone. When they are very hungry, lions in the Kalahari will even eat porcupines, although they can die from wounds caused by the quills. Sometimes lions will also steal kills from other predators, especially hyenas.

Both African and Asiatic lions live in fairly close contact with humans and will often kill and eat farm animals, such as goats and sheep.

A group of very full lions doze after a meal. Lions and lionesses are active only when they need to be and may spend over 20 hours each day lying around.

A male lion in the Serengeti National Park, in Tanzania. African people used to kill a small number of lions. They ate their meat and turned their manes and skins into clothes.

Lions & Man

Africans have long had a close relationship with the lions that share the land on which they live. In the past, they used to hunt lions, using spears, nets, and traps. But they took only enough for their needs. Then, about 100 years ago, lion hunting for sport became popular among the European settlers in Africa. These people had guns, which could kill lions much more easily than spears could. Since then, many lions have been wiped out. As we have seen, one subspecies is now totally extinct, and another is extinct in the wild. Over the years the numbers of the other African subspecies have also fallen. In 1950, there were thought to be about 400,000 lions in Africa. Today there are just 100,000 left.

The Asiatic lion has also disappeared from much of its range. Asiatic lions are mainly at risk from loss of habitat, as people take more and more land on which to build their homes and farms. Added to this, many farmers shoot lions on sight because they kill their cattle. Sometimes lions even attack people. Between 1988 and 1990, a drought in India killed many farm animals, and the lions took to feeding on humans. Generally, however, lions do not attack people unless they are too old or sick to catch their normal prey.

These lion and leopard skins are on sale as souvenirs in Kenya. The skins of big cats killed as pests may be sold as long as the dealer gets special permission.

Saving Lions

The hunting that was once so widespread has now been banned, and people travel to Africa to take pictures of wild animals rather than to shoot them with guns. As well as being protected from hunting by law, most African lions live in reserves and national parks, such as the Masai Mara Game Reserve and the Serengeti National Park.

Asiatic lions are also protected from hunting and land development in their **sanctuary** in the Gir Forest in India, which was set up in the early 1970s. In 1974 there were only 180 Asiatic lions left in the wild, and the situation was extremely serious. Since then, their numbers have been rising slowly but steadily inside the reserve. There were

In order to protect lions, scientists need to know as much about them as possible. This lioness wears a radio collar, so that her movements can be tracked.

205 Asiatic lions in the Gir Forest in 1979, 239 in 1985, 284 in 1990, and in 1995 there were 304. If this success is to continue and the size of the population is to keep increasing, the lions will need more space. There are plans to build a second sanctuary or extend the boundaries of the present one into the surrounding areas.

There are problems with having all the lions living in one area. The main one is that they can breed only with one another, since there are no male lions anywhere else to come in and take over the prides. The regular arrival of new males from other families is important for a healthy

"Not so fast!" A lioness keeps a close watch on a cub as it trots across an African game reserve. Tourists are watching from the safety of their vehicles.

A young lion cub sucks milk from a bottle. There are plenty of lions in zoos around the world. Many of these are crosses between either Asiatic lions and a subspecies of African lion or between two African subspecies.

population. In addition, if a deadly disease were to arrive in the Gir sanctuary, it could kill all the wild Asiatic lions at one time. For these reasons, the government of Gujarat has decided to move some lions from the Gir sanctuary to two other parks – in the states of Madhya Pradesh in central India and Rajasthan in the north.

North American zoos are also taking a hand in protecting the Asiatic lion. Zoos belonging to the American Zoo and Aquarium Association have a special program called a Species Survival Plan (SSP). In this program, pure

Asiatic lions are bred and raised in **captivity** so that if all the wild lions die out, there will still be some Asiatic lions left in the world. Since 1993, there has been an SSP for African lions as well. This program aims to breed lions of each of the African subspecies, and so far it has more than 30 Transvaal lions. **Conservationists** have to be careful which lions they choose, though. Only purebred lions will do for the programs, and many zoo lions are crosses.

As long as people do not begin hunting lions on a large scale again, the future for both African and Asiatic lions looks good. And if reserves and national parks can remain safe for wildlife and untouched by humans, the beautiful, majestic lion may be saved after all.

Scientists and many other people are working hard to save lions. Thanks to their efforts, the "king of the beasts" and his kind may still have a future in the wild.

Useful Addresses

For more information about lions and how you can help protect them, contact these organizations:

African Wildlife Foundation
1717 Massachusetts Avenue NW
Suite 602
Washington, D.C. 20036

Elsa Wild Animal Appeal – USA
P.O. Box 675
Elmhurst, Illinois 60126

Kenya Wildlife Fund
P.O. Box 2445, Station B
Richmond Hill
Ontario L4E 1A5

U.S. Fish and Wildlife Service
Endangered Species and Habitat
Conservation
400 Arlington Square
18th and C Streets NW
Washington, D.C. 20240

Wildlife Preservation Trust International
3400 W. Girard Avenue
Philadelphia, PA 19104

World Wildlife Fund
1250 24th Street NW
Washington, D.C. 20037

Further Reading

The African Lion Carl R. Green (New York: Crestwood House, 1987)

Amazing Cats Alexandra Parsons (New York: Alfred A. Knopf, 1990)

Animals in Danger Marcus Schneck (New York: Gallery Books, 1990)

Big Cats Norman Barrett (New York: Franklin Watts, 1990)

Endangered Animals Steve Pollock (New York: Facts On File, 1993)

Endangered Wildlife of the World (New York: Marshall Cavendish Corporation, 1993)

Lions Leslie McGuire (New York: Atheneum, 1989)

Lions and Tigers and Leopards: The Big Cats Jennifer C. Urquhart (Washington, D.C.: National Geographic Society, 1991)

Wildlife of the World (New York: Marshall Cavendish Corporation, 1994)

Glossary

Adapt: To change in order to survive in new conditions.

Captivity: Confinement; for animals, usually in a cage.

Carnivore: A meat-eating animal.

Conservationist (Kon-ser-VAY-shun-ist): A person who protects and preserves the Earth's natural resources, such as animals, plants, and soil.

Extinct (Ex-TINKT): No longer living anywhere in the world.

Habitat: The place where an animal lives. For example, the Asiatic lion's habitat is the forest.

Lair: A safe place where a lioness gives birth to her cubs.

Mammal: A kind of animal that is warm-blooded and has a backbone. Most mammals are covered with fur or have hair. Females have glands that produce milk to feed their young.

Mate: When a male and female get together to produce young.

Predator: A kind of animal that hunts and eats other animals.

Prey: An animal that is hunted and eaten by another animal.

Pride: The name given to a group of lions that live together.

Range: The area in the world in which a particular species of animal can be found.

Reserve: Land that has been set aside where plants and animals can live without being harmed.

Sanctuary (SANK-chu-wer-ee): A safe place.

Scrub: Land that is covered by low trees and shrubs.

Species: A kind of animal or plant. For example, the lion is a species of cat.

Subspecies: A group within a species. The Asiatic lion is a subspecies of lion.

Territory: The piece of land in which a group of animals lives. Lions defend their territory against others of their own kind.

Tropical: Having to do with or found in the tropics, the warm region of the Earth near the Equator.

Index